Hyacinth for the Soul

Poems by
Joan I. Siegel

For Lucille & Stu...
a Hyacinth for the Soul
for you!

much love,
Joan
(7·10·12)

DEERBROOK EDITIONS 2009

PUBLISHED BY
Deerbrook Editions
P.O. Box 542
Cumberland, ME 04021
207-829-5038

FIRST EDITION

ISBN:
0-9712488-9-3
978-0-9712488-9-2

On the cover:
Alzheimer Thoughts (1991), quilt by Susan Heller,
copyright by Susan Heller

Book design by Jeffrey Haste

Contents

I

13 The Bronx
14 Space Time Travel
15 Memory
16 1950
17 The Horse
19 Key
20 Sleep Walker
21 January Thaw
22 Perennial
23 Savings

II

27 Eurydice in the Underworld
31 Travel Directions
32 First Words
33 Wild Columbine
34 How We Look After Each Other
35 Bedside
36 Washing My Daughter's Hair
37 Thomas Hart Benton: Persephone (1939)
38 Hyacinth for the Soul
39 Imago
40 Night Travel
41 Lager
42 Rag Man of Middletown
43 Glass
44 Night School
45 Dorothea Lange: Migrant Mother (1936)
46 Daughters
47 To My Husband

III

51 War Photo
52 Christ on the Cross
53 Ceres
54 Outlawed
55 Hiroshima
56 Haggadah
58 The Great Masters
59 On the Sudden Death of a Friend
60 Suicide in the Pennsylvania Woods
61 Beethoven: Les Adieux
62 Failed Magic
63 Talking to the Blind & Deaf Dog at Night

IV

67 Piano Lesson
68 Folk Tale
69 The Mother of Joan of Arc
70 Mary Cassatt: The Letter (1890-1)
71 How the Turtle Knew It Was Her Time
72 Blood
73 Burial
74 Cat
75 Listening to Bach's Mass in B-Minor
76 Chopin Prelude in E-Minor
77 Playing Clair de Lune on My Mother's Birthday
78 Winter Solstice
79 On the Night Train to Marseilles

For My Family

Hyacinth for the Soul

I

We knew who we were back then
at ease in our parents' folding chairs
outside the corner drugstore.

You with your pink cat's-eyes
sunglasses, rhinestone-studded.
Me with a candy cigarette hanging

from my lower lip. Exhaling
invisible smoke and rocking
my doll to sleep just like the real

mothers on our block. The ones
on the front stoop with frothy
laughter and scolding tongues.

Long before doubt crept up
like a pickpocket and snatched
the keys to our house,

we'd gotten it all down: style
lingo, all the verities. Snug
as our feet in square-toed socks.

Eyes shut tight
we talked ourselves to sleep
about where the sky ends
and rocketed out of bed across
the galaxy

heedless of dark matter
dark energy
black holes that could vacuum us
up like a pair of socks.

We traveled so fast
our years blew off like lint.

We grew smaller
back to un-conception:
particles of anti-matter
quarks
invisible as our future.

As though darkness were a hand,
a tactile memory
like playing the piano.
You touch lost things:
The texture of green walls
in the living room where you lived.
Walls green as a forest at midnight
of the new moon. How a stain
on the ceiling was a bird's wing
in the shadows of the table lamp. You
and your sister on the floor playing jacks,
comfortable as animals in each other's
smell. The iron radiator hissing
steam, warming
the room while winter
scored its breath on the window
pane. In the kitchen, voices
of mother and father. Out of nowhere
the notion they could die. Later
the broiler's red
hot wire. How the veins
of the lamb on your plate looked
just like the veins in your wrist.

What I remember has texture
like the grainy feel of a black and white
photograph. Your eyes are lucid and honest
as the blue glass stone in your locket. We are
sitting at a wooden table in the living
room. It could be a winter afternoon. Venetian blinds
stripe the floor with sunlight. Our mother and
father are elsewhere off camera. You are
embroidering in one of those pink plastic frames.
I am cutting construction paper with dull-edged
scissors. We hear the prick of the needle
in the muslin, the cutting of the paper,
the hiss of the radiator—
but the hours' passing has its own sound,
its own iron taste in the mouth,
its own deepening light. The green walls
of the living room darken
like a forest. We could be
two lost children far
from home.

To save us forever they said,
If that old horse climbs up on the sidewalk
watch out! He'll swallow you whole.
I was five in the summer streets.

If that old horse climbs up on the sidewalk
dragging the peddler's wagon load of melons.
I was five in the summer streets.
I knew his wet eyes looking at me

dragging the peddler's wagon load of melons.
The plums were dark as night in the afternoon.
I knew his wet eyes looking at me.
Iron bit in his gums. Teeth grinning.

The plums were dark as night that afternoon
he waited at the curbside, whinnied to the sun.
Iron bit in his mouth. Teeth grinning.
I touched his flanks. I kissed his dusty mane.

He waited at the curbside, whinnied to the sun
while they reached for bags full of juicy plums.
I touched his flanks. I kissed his dusty mane.
The harness rattled. The wagon creaked.

They reached for bags full of juicy plums.
He shifted his weight, one hoof in the air.
The harness rattled. The wagon creaked.
I smelled his smell on my hands, my face.

He shifted his weight, one hoof in the air.
Melons bounced. Plums rolled in the gutter.
I smelled his smell on my hands, my face.
My heart jumped high in its ivory cage.

Melons bounced. Plums rolled in the gutter.
Dizzy down the street with love and fear,
my heart jumped high in its ivory cage.
I hid behind a cellar door and cried.

Dizzy down the street with love and fear,
Watch out! He'll swallow you whole!
I hid behind a cellar door and cried.
As if that could save me.

In the photograph, circa 1939,
they are standing beside a train.
She wears a summer dress,
a broad white hat. His arm
is slipped through hers.
They are young.

I still have the key,
but it won't unlock the house
where they lived and died:

My father dark as rain
on black umbrellas.

My mother in the kitchen
sipping cold tea.

Separate
locked rooms.

They asked a stranger
to take the picture.

Where
were they going?

My father gets out of bed, unlocks
three deadbolts on the apartment door
and rides the elevator to the street.
He wears a pair of cotton pajama pants.
His shoes are upstairs in the closet.
Upstairs too my mother sleeps beside
his empty place in the bed. The lights
are out in all the stores, the window
shades pulled. My father walks
barefoot around the neighborhood
like one of those lost old men
you expect to meet in a story
by I. B. Singer. Like them, he is traveling
a nightmare. He isn't watching his children fly
out the chimney in Birkenau. Still
his brain is raveling skein by skein,
the threads don't trail the way home.
So when the police find him hours
later, he says he is out looking
for the folks. They take him to the address
on his ID bracelet. At the door,
my mother stands in her bathrobe,
crying. "So where'd you go?" she asks.
"Who are you?" he answers.

This winter sunshine loosens time.
I shut my eyes and let it be
the park, the boy from nursery school.
Inside the earth our fingers dig
where earth is chill and all around
the sun soaks through our woolen coats
and on our mud-slick hands. We are
the smell of mud and sun and worms.
Impatiently we pull them up
to curl the air and whip the ground
and crisp our upturned palms. When they
twist back inside the dark, the sun
rolls down and with it fifty years
contract and stiffen, stern as bone.

While we slept last night,
late October frost passed
over the garden like the angel
of death, shriveling
the purple heads of cone flowers.

Already the smell of snow.
Tightening in the ribs.

Little by little,
afternoons shrink around us
in the darkening rooms. Inexorable,
the earth's engines drive headlong.

Deer huddle in their yards.
Black bears sleep. Tree frogs
suspend. All
abide.

Elsewhere, someone
is opening a door,
stepping out in the garden
where the first crocus pushes up
like the fingers of Persephone
eager for light.

Here, we tap in the dark, call
to each other.

Against that time when my life
is an empty room,
drawn blinds and a night light—

      I stuff my suitcase with this
Sunday morning when you are still
eleven years old in your red and black
penguin pajamas, reading a library book
and both of us and your favorite cat burrow
inside an old sleeping bag while busily
your father snores under the bed sheets and last
week's snow is thick in the woods where later
we'll snowshoe through fresh deer tracks in
a brush painting of black branches.

            Already I have pocketed
your songs and laughter, pushed them deep
against the seams of my palm, the map
out of darkness.

II

i

The night before our wedding
I dreamed I woke in a forest of cypress:
all the oak were gone
the laurel
beech and hazel
all the linden
all the silver fir
as if you'd called them away
leaving only the cypress
the tree that mourns.

Far off I heard you singing.
The cypress prayed.

You sang my name
and I walked to the edge of the dream,
a meadow sunny with asphodel and phlox
and a snake sank its poison in my heel.
The cypress moaned.
The meadow went soft like a sea
and I drowned.

ii

They say you're coming back for me.

I must
grow flesh on my bones
cell by cell
rethread my veins   my nerves my brain
make blood

make ears and lips
and eyes
open my eyes again
and walk into light with you.

I must be pieced together
a quilt of memories
stitched with words we used to speak.

iii

It is all so new
this white flesh
the weight of breasts
how fingers bend.
I've lain beneath the roots of trees so long
the roots groan through my hair.

I try to remember
green that spreads above loam
what grows upward to the sky
the sky
the smell of the sky.

I try to hear your singing
that stills rocks   trees   wild beasts
my heart wild
to feel again the weight of you
your taste.

Instead I hear the sound
of mould spreading in the hollow
mouths of the dead.
My eyes are dry as bark.

Why make me desire
what I have lost forever
in this place where there is nothing
but silence
worse than anything you know
who can hear your own breathing
and the hum of poems about love & death.

iv

I followed you through pitch and
worminess
limping from that old wound
up steep rocks slippery with lichen
dripping on hollow eyes below.

But even before we passed Avernus,
even before you looked back,
I saw the shaft of blue light
from the world I lost:

I had forgotten blue
how it smells of rain
how it colors wild lupine and
bellflowers of the field
the breast feathers of birds
the veins in my wrist
the sweet air where our life had been.

The light scorched my eyes.
It burned the new skin of my face.
All the while the dead
shrill in my ears.
I tried to speak.

There ought to be a word
for the way you know how to get some place
but don't remember the names of streets
the number of turns and blinking yellow lights
so that if someone asked
you really couldn't say
except you know the road starts out straight
and when it's sunny the branches blink across
the windshield making you want to rub your eyes
then the road turns sharply uphill past a red barn
where a black dog jumps out to race you for a quarter mile
and finally recedes in the mirror like a disappointment
and you remember the road dips downhill
into the shadows of the morning
where you hear Bach's unaccompanied 'cello
and understand what a good fit the 'cello makes
in the hollow of the body
where grief begins and for an indeterminate time
the road winds vaguely past
houses   people   road signs
while time hums in your ear and you remember
the dream you left behind that morning
which had nothing
to do with where
you are going

The way each word pushes through your lips
sometimes makes me think of the birth of a foal
who squeezes through the dark
a little misshapen and folded
trying to stand on wobbly legs and shake
himself open.

Sometimes you make me think
of a fish feeding on water as you suck in a breath
and out float words like bubbles.

Sometimes you make me think of a glassblower
with his puffy cheeks and eyes squeezed almost shut
intent on the shape turning in the flame.

In the frozen ground under my feet
the wild columbine
neither patient nor impatient
curls up like a thought
before the words that name it.
And there it rests
until one warm afternoon in spring
when I have other things on my mind
it rises through the dead leaves.

Toward the end
I carried him like a baby
through my dreams. I worried
I'd lose him in the crowds.
Now he visits my sleep.
Dying was the easy thing,
he says, then drives off
in his 1940 Studebaker.
They say after a death
someone unexpected
comes. This black cat,
for instance, who strayed
from the woods, looking
disheveled and lost,
the way my father wandered
the streets, barefoot
weeping for his family—
not knowing
he'd found us.

At the edge
her legs
thin as tree roots
hanging above a river
thirst for the icy
current to pull her
into the fish shoals
drag her through weeds
to the soft sand
the wrinkled bed sheets
of the river bottom
where at last she can lie still
letting the water fill her mouth
and ears
close her eyes
and see
daylight shattering
the water's surface
the way a crystal bowl
once fell from her hands
onto the kitchen floor

Supple as willow curved above a stream,
she perches on a bench, rounds her shoulders,
tosses silken hair over the kitchen sink.

I lather the black heft in my hands.
Warm water runs through our laughter
and the soapy fragrance of the morning.

She sings, wipes suds from her eyes.

The exposed neck,
its feathered down,
the rounded back,
shoulders sharp as sparrow wings

already it is here in abeyance—
loneliness,
hollow bones.

She is picking some violets and white lilies.
It is a cool mossy place in the woods
near the house. The air buzzes the way it does

on a hot summer afternoon in Missouri.
She stretches out along a tree stump to rest
her head buzzing with the things teenage girls

think about. She never hears him come:
the old farmer with his plowman's hands
groping at her blouse, ripping the seams,

buttons popping like seed pods
on the ground. She screams for her mother
and the things in her head scatter

like scared birds in the branches. The sky
goes white as he drags her down into the moss
and bracken flooding her with himself. Then

he leaves her there. Before she gets up on her feet
again and walks back home, she buries herself
alive under the leaves and dirt.

Bake two loaves of bread, my mother used to say.
Give one away and plant a hyacinth for the soul.
I never understood and she did not explain.
It was one of those sayings from the old country.

Give one away and plant a hyacinth for the soul
as if the soul would not prefer two loaves of bread.
It was one of those sayings from the old country
that my Polish grandmother passed on to her daughters.

As if the soul would not prefer two loaves of bread
hungry and alone in its room beneath the heart,
that my Polish grandmother passed on to her daughters:
Oh, soul who are you? What do you know?

Hungry and alone in my room beneath the heart,
I sit out the bruised hours wondering,
Oh, soul who are you? What do you know?
until a poem rises through the dead leaves. Flowers.

I sit out the bruised hours wondering
who are the faces in the photographs
until words rise through the dry leaves. Flower.
I kneel in the dirt, plant hyacinths for my mother.

Who are the faces in the photographs?
I never understood and she did not explain.
So I kneel in the dirt, plant hyacinths for my mother,
bake two loaves of bread as she used to say.

It worms its back
of tufted witch's warts
along the ground
grows fat on thistles
meadow peas   mallow
bursts its spiny green and yellow skin

then spins itself
to sleep
sheathed in green silk
a wrinkled leaf
suspended by a single
thread

rearranges itself
like a girl trying on
her mother's clothes
putting on lipstick   mascara

steps out
a Painted Lady
winged light
in the asters

What is it climbs my sleep
in the middle of this summer night?
Insistent as a cat, it settles
on the pillow, breathing
next to my face, urging

me to sleepwalk up the attic steps
to fumble with locks, push open a door
to cold weather, the sky's blue-black
skin frozen on the window
pane. Here clocks tumble

from cartons beside my first pair
of shoes and 100 seasons shed
like silk. In my ear is a phone
call from my father who always
said, *Keep your wits about you*

because he worried about us
when he wasn't around any longer.
Then the earth spins leaving my father
behind and I am late again
for a piano lesson, my right hand practicing

Brahms inside my coat pocket, my eyes
looking down the subway tracks long after
midnight for the train that won't come, afraid
of that man leaning against the tiled
wall, and my feet too heavy to run.

He is a dray animal,
his belly empty as the mind.
Time is the iron harness
that drags him through mud.
How fast can he trot? A voice
barks at his heels. A language
he doesn't understand. He used
to be a man. He had a wife.
He had two daughters. One son.
Once he had a mother and father.
Long ago in another country
he had a childhood. He played
on the streets with friends. The
old peddler drove up in his wagon
and tossed him a ripe peach.

In Buchenwald
his sister turned into a bird
and flew out the chimney stack.

In America
he found a wife,
then lost her.

An old man with sooty eyes
and sooty pants, he steers
a baby carriage brimming

with rags. Here and there
on the roadside, he bows low
to passing cars. Tips the hat

he isn't wearing. Bends
in the weeds to pick cloth
for the emperor's new clothes.

A bird flies into the window
as if the sky had dropped
and made a dull sound.

Summer nights
moths fly to the light
beating their wings into madness
and the madness melts into silver
threads on the glass.

Trains
pull out of lonely stations
smelling of diesel and steam.
On each window
the slow streaking of faces.

In a classroom like this one where
her children once sat fidgeting
for the bell to ring so they could grab
their jackets and shout to the cold air and sun
shining on Broadway two blocks from home
where two flights up she had set out bread
and milk on the kitchen table because
she was down the street at the tailor's shop
turning a shirt collar or mending a man's coat
and nights she got down on her hands and knees
to wash floors in an office building on Second Avenue
things she had learned as a girl in Poland
and brought with her a boat ride away to Ellis Island
to the man she married and soon enough
their four children (one dead)
and after he died of influenza
to the new husband and his five children (one dead)
and in time to the new daughters-in-law
and sons-in-law in their uptown apartments
and the babies one at a time
she sat practicing her Palmer letters
connecting the fine threads of ink
each graceful curve looping to the next
like crocheting a pair of ladies gloves
making words where silence used to be.

After the peas freeze on the vine,
they feed on wild birds.
Then they feed on dust.

Hunger grows fat
on their flesh.
It climbs up their sleep
into their eyes.

She sits in the roadside tent,
a lookout
still as bark.
Her ears are caves
rattling with ice and wind.

She sells the truck tires
for food.
There is no reprieve,
nowhere to go.

The children wrap
around her like a shawl,
too big to crawl back in.

> "... may we carry our mothers forth in our bellies."
> —*Maxine Kumin*

We carry our mother's death inside us
as she carried us
but we are not delivered of it
this heaviness
we bear it all our lives
underneath our breath
at the bottom of our laughter
it is there when we rise in the morning
and bend over our sleeping child at night
a dark thing
dark as the bureau drawer
where beneath sheets of pale tissue paper
we keep the crocheted gloves aged the color of tea
the silk scarves
the beaded handbag
we see fingers threading the beads
we hear the snap of thread

In your family
everyone left
without saying
a word.

Your father
took a bus
to the VA hospital
& died quietly
on the front steps.

Your mother
curled up
in intensive care
& bled to death from the mouth.

Your brother
slammed the door shut
& walked away.

You
must not believe—
all these years after
that winter afternoon
when we were like children
together for the first time—
I will ever let you
walk out of this house
into the dark woods
alone.

III

Nearby flows Euphrates,
the fourth river that *went out of Eden*
to water the garden.

The four year old wears a pink jacket
the color of apple blossom sprayed
with her mother's blood.

The marine's eyes are half-moons.
His face is the darkness of a father
holding a dying child.

In the beginning
darkness was the only face
and God said:

Let there be light
and light was divided from darkness,
so we would know one from the other.

It is private
this howling of a man's body
and yet we push through the crowd
the way we push our chair up close
to the evening news
to watch
hot blood sputtering
from iron nails driven
through hands and feet
to watch skin flapping
like a torn pocket
beneath the breast
to watch wrists
hips unlocking
muscles twisting
off bones   tendons
snapping like rubber bands
to watch the spine separating
from itself knot
by knot
to watch the mouth open
eyes rolling toward heaven
nerves dangling
like live wires.

From the Plaza de Mayo
to the mountain passes and
back streets of Sarajevo
the carpet shops of Morocco
and Bangladesh
the sex marts of Bangkok
she scours the earth searching
for a discarded shoe
a sweater button
crumpled paper with her handwriting
a hair clip
anything left behind to prove
she was there—
one blighted village after another
one withered field after another
on her tongue the dust
of her daughter's name.

The woman with a raccoon's face.
A birthmark stretches across her eyes.
It fits like a mask. When she looks up,
she does not look at you. Her legs
are swollen, wrapped in rags. Her nose
leans close to the ground as if tracking a scent.

All night she burrows beneath the city
among the outlawed. Crouched in darkness,
beside the iron tracks, the rust
and drip of drainage pipes. What news,
what vision sends her up the long,
slow stairs? The sidewalk shines. The sky

is blue. A trash can brims with goodness.
She stops. She talks to her wire cart.

The woman says:
> Everyone ran to the river
> and jumped in.
> There I found my father,
> a miracle.
> We floated downstream
> with all the burning dead.

The man says:
> I was playing soldier outside
> when a great flash shook the sky
> and the house dropped on my sister.
> She screamed *Help me! Help me!*
> but I couldn't pull her out. Then the fires
> came, the wind came. Our neighbors
> took me away.

The old man says:
> I was a miracle.
> I did not burn.

The blind woman says:
> In this bed
> I sleep and wake
> every day
> darkness begins
> the wind catches fire.

If not death

                    still there would be winter

If not winter
that burns a man's lips blue
and freezes excrement and blood
winter that roars through cloth
slashes the weft of flesh
the warp of sleep

                    still there would be hunger

If not hunger
growling like a wild beast
in the empty belly
in the bones
in the eyes
in the ears

                    still there would be fear

If not fear
in the eyes of the mothers
in the eyes of the fathers
in the eyes of the daughters
in the eyes of the sons
all eyes
crawling in the mud
slouching toward nothing

                    still there would be hope

If not hope
when the spring rains came
and washed the air
and washed the earth
and washed the fire

and washed the blood
and punished all with memory
so that one might recall
he was once a man

            still there would be shame

If not shame
for what one has thought
or not thought
shame for what one has done
or not done
shame for what one has become
or not become
among the living
and the dead

            still there would be death

And if not death

            still there would be memory

In the paintings of the great masters
a woman is usually naked, stepping
into the bathtub or just out of it. Water glistens
on her breasts. She bends like a branch to wring out
her long, thick hair. You can hear the master's breath.
Another time she is with her sisters
splashing naked in some pond
in the middle of the woods. Or they dance
together around the trees. They don't know
they are being watched.
She sits naked at a picnic on the grass
with some well-dressed Victorian gentlemen
or in a meadow by herself daydreaming
in the artist's dappled light.
At home she stretches out on the couch
as though she has nothing else to do—naked and
bejeweled at mid-afternoon, surrounded
by bowls of ripe grapes and pears, or peacocks.
The maid stands by with flowers.
Sometimes she sits at the mirror,
wearing garters or wearing nothing at all,
simply brushing her hair,
or she undresses herself,
pulls off a stocking,
unwraps a skirt,
as if she were finally alone in her room
at the end of the day. She doesn't hear
that other woman screaming in the next gallery—
the one thrown to the ground,
hair trussed by the roots,
clothes ripped from her body,
trampled naked and torn by thundering
gods and satyrs
and all the king's men.

Deer on the snow:
hunger and beauty.

I step back to gain
perspective
                    as yesterday
I stepped back
from the telephone announcing
your death.
                    Such heaviness
left at my door. How to lift it?
Where to lay it down?

I phone your house. The message
begins. Your voice says
you are not there.

Suicide in the Pennsylvania Woods   (for Huguette)

Did she keep her eyes open?
Did she close them?

Did she see her whole life
or only the hem of her skirt?

Did a branch of cedar remind her of
the birthmark on her son's leg?

Did the January wind make her pull up
her collar, turn back toward home?

Did the icy metal startle her finger?
Did her thoughts scatter like wild birds in a storm?

Did someone else hear it?
Did it travel far before it was nothing?

Did the coldness come first to her eyes,
then her heart?

Did the snow bleed?
Did the sky blacken with crows?

Did Shadow the Great Dane
bolt, lick wildly her face?

The treachery of roads and war.
Farewell. So far as eyes can see
the gentle rise of Alpine hills,
Carpathians that pierce the sky:
so far does desolation reach.
This absence is winter. A keyboard of ice,

black trees carved bare, a sudden cleft
where one could slip forever lost
among the frozen nests of birds.
One hears the sadness in dead things.
How loneliness pulls down the shades
and time keeps time in an empty room.

Clouds press against the windowpane,
the wind even sings in a minor key.

I stayed awake
saying magic words
to the darkness
one hundred times
so that the four-year-old
girl in the schoolyard would not
die of a baseball hitting
her *solar plexus*—
a part of the body
I'd never heard of before—
and *die* was what happened
to our fish that floated on its side
at the top of the tank
looking straight up
with one astonished eye
and later someone scooped it out
so it was *gone forever*
which they said I'd understand
when I grew up

After the house is quiet you take the dog out
in the late night woods when the winter moon
looks on like a blind eye among the branches.

The air is still, snow crunches underfoot,
the dog doesn't hear. Maybe he turns around
to smell that you are still behind him.

There's always the matter of love.
He wants to see you. You tell him a memory.
Whatever comes to mind. It doesn't matter.

You live your life in the order that things happen
but afterwards it comes to you out of sequence
—one moment or another refracted through time

like a chip of broken glass. You see how it fits together.
Then darkness. The dog understands darkness.
He stops, pricks up his ears.

IV

Then it was winter.
Heavy with snow, the sky
pressed against the window
and your old teacher bent
his head listening to you
play Bach. The landscape
was rigid. Exact. You could cut
your fingers on its ivory edge.

Later, in the street, you lifted
your face to the snow and
loved the lamp post, the sky,
your life.

The childless farmer's wife dreams
about the cow and her calf. Warm milk
squeezed through her fingers into a pail.
She rends her apron and prays. Each night
she makes deals with the gods.

         She'd give back anything—
Her mother's gold ring.
Her mother's last words.
The years of her childhood.
Her long golden hair.
The first night of love.
One arm, two eyes,
all her memories,

even the calf's tongue on the udder,
the sound of sucking in the warm barn,
the smell of fresh straw.

She walks one hundred miles
to kneel at the statue of Mary.

In Le Puy's cold cathedral,
she prays for her daughter,
one mother to another.

Her prayer
is the mother's longing—
as it was at the birth
that first ripped her open—
to hold
what her body made

not see the flesh
of her flesh
burn
like paper.

All day it is with her like a song
even as she slices a breakfast orange,
brushes her hair,
shuts a window.
She is listening to it
when company calls
and she talks about yesterday's news,
pours tea,
says good bye at the door.
Then alone with it finally
in late afternoon,
she puts it on the desk,
arranges it
as though she were putting flowers in a vase.
Then she slips it into the envelope,
seals it with her tongue.

Did the sun dip into the water this morning
staining it with blood, an omen
while the moon looked away
or is it how the water moved and didn't move
around the water lilies or how the lichen spread
over the rocks or because of a sudden agitation
in the beating of the dragon flies' wings or how
the day lilies spread open and shut or something
in the blue of the Sweet Williams reminded her of winter
and loneliness edged downward from her belly
so that she heaved herself out of the pond
and up the steep roadside to dig the hole
where she sits now
still and purposeful as if to say,
it suffices.

This morning a missile exploded
their house. His sister and brother went up
with the windows and chairs. Then
sister and brother rained on his face.

Now he sits on the hospital floor. Waiting.
His mother so still, her face
turned his way on the gurney. Her blood
finds his on the floor.

Long before he was born, their river
of blood was one. She told him—
when the world was a still place,
she'd heard it murmuring through them.

He leaves only the body that has failed him—
a house robbed of its treasure, the eerie
silence after thieves have fled. Tongue
and bone, the brain's light years of travel
swept into a parcel small as a shoebox
and into a hole too narrow
for his broad shoulders.

Where is the music
when the dark piano lid is shut?

He does not wait for the sun's return.
Instead he makes a pillow of darkness
to stretch inside this longest night.
To burrow deep as if it were
the foot of the bed, his rightful place
for twenty years beside our sleep.

His eyes alert and green as wide
savannahs where his kind began.
From time to time his head rears up
to roar at pain, then lowers it
to listen. Teaching us who'd hold
him back the way of animals—

his body patient with itself,
unlocking slowly cell by cell.

Carved like a cathedral
this music of redemption

spires above the human soul
weighted with the things

of this world in a universe
scientists imagine

began with a primal tone
like the hum of an organ stop

resonating in the nothing that was
at the beginning. There is

no safety. The moth pupa suspended
in its chrysalis

the impala circled by lions
at the watering hole. How simple

to roll off the earth into the night
and dissolve among the stars.

This page missing from the book of preludes
with their spiraling descents and
breaks of sudden weather
this quiet page missing ten years
folded in my father's hand
to take along on the journey
as if the dead really need what we give them
this music in a minor key
the mode of mourning
I know by heart
I feel it in my fingers
as I feel the sleeve of his gray sweater
what is part of me
his knees, his funny walk
the way his eyes look far away
I can summon it any time at the piano
this meditation
my father listening in his armchair
there by the window

Does moonlight sift through stone and touch her hands
the way it settled in my sleep when I
was six years old, entangled in bad dreams
as dark as grief that slipped like river grass

around my arms and feet, and bound my neck
so when I called out loud my voice went deaf.
The river swallowed me and I was lost
among the empty ears of shells. It seemed

my hands dissolved. My fingers curled away
like schools of fish. But in the flashing shoals,
I saw the watery moon and breathlessly
I reached along its twisting current home,

swam up the moonlight she began to play:
that shaft of music from the living room.

This light,
heavy as the weft
of darkness
in a Bach fugue,
makes you remember
the deaths of forgotten things—
sparrow bones
buried in the backyard,
a doll whose eye
went blind,
pansies fallen from a book
dry and purple as a wound.

You wrap night around
you like a house
where you sit looking
out the window
with the illusion
that walls, floor,
ceiling are solid
as the spinning earth tilted
away from the sun
your eye searching the horizon
your ear pressed
to the pedal point
waiting
for it to give way
to brightness.

Through your reflection in the window,
a woman embraces a man in the light
of the station. You only glimpse their story
as the wheels push them into shadow.
You slide into night farther from home,
the past unbending along the track.

You shut your eyes to keep track
of forgotten things: the window
that opened to a pear tree at home,
how the room flooded with light
and high up on the walls, a shadow
told its own story.

You don't remember the story.
Instead you look down the track
to the man and woman in shadow
who slipped past your window.
How you'd watched in the yellow light
separate, feeling sick for home.

But where is home?
You never know their story
as you never discovered the source of light
or found a way to track
it from the pear tree near the window.
What was inside the shadow?

Between stations a man falls into the shadow.
They bring a coffin, carry him home.
You watch by the window.
He has a name, a favorite umbrella, a story.
He leaves a shoe beside the track
just as morning light

gives shape to memory. In the weak light
the dead man is shapeless. A shadow
on your memory that will track
you all the years you are home-
less. At the end of the last story,
the pear tree taps at the window.

You stand at the dark window. Light
a candle. Your story is the shadow
following you home along the track.

Acknowledgments

Grateful acknowledgment is made to the editors and publishers of magazines in which these poems (some in earlier versions) first appeared:

Alaska Quarterly Review "Blood," "Talking to the Blind & Deaf Dog at Night"; *The American Scholar* "First Words"; *The Amicus Journal* "How the Turtle Knew It Was Her Time," "Wild Columbine"; *The Atlantic Monthly* "Mary Cassatt: The Letter"; *Bellevue Literary Review* "Cat"; *Chautauqua Literary Journal* "Playing Clair de Lune on My Mother's Birthday"; *Commonweal* "Bedside," "Burial," "Dorothea Lange: Migrant Mother," "Hiroshima," "Hyacinth for the Soul," "Perennial," "Sleep Walker," "The Mother of Joan of Arc"; *The Connecticut Review* "The Bronx," "Folk Tale"; *Free Lunch* "Imago," "Space Time Travel," "Travel Directions"; *The Gettysburg Review* "The Great Masters," "Listening to Bach's Mass in B-Minor"; *The Hampden-Sydney Poetry Review* "Winter Solstice"; *Journal of Genocide Research* "Haggadah"; *The Literary Review* "Piano Lesson"; *Margie* "How We Look After Each Other," "Key," "Lager," "On the Sudden Death of a Friend"; *Natural Bridge* "Thomas Hart Benton: Persephone"; *New Letters* "Chopin Prelude in E Minor," "Daughters," "Eurydice in the Underworld"; *The North American Review* "Washing My Daughter's Hair"; *Northeast* "Glass"; *Poetry East* "Ceres," "Savings," "To My Husband"; *Poet Lore* "1950," "Night Travel"; *Potomac Review* "January Thaw," "War Photo"; *Prairie Schooner* "Night School," "The Horse," *Rattle* "Memory"; *Rhino* "Suicide in the Pennsylvania Woods"; *Tar River Poetry* "Christ on the Cross"; and *Witness* "Failed Magic," "Outlawed," "Rag Man of Middletown".

86

Special thanks to Rosemary Deen, Rita Gabis, Rachel Hadas, Jeffrey Haste, Susan and Jack Heller, Maxine Kumin, Mary Makofske, Frances Richey, Mindy Ross, Vivian Shipley, William Trowbridge, Diane Wakoski, and my family.

Notes:
 Both "Lager" and "Haggadah" were inspired by the works of Primo Levi.
 "Blood" is based on a photograph by Kael Alford in *Unembedded: Four Independent Photojournalists on the War in Iraq*.
 "War Photo" is based on a photograph in *The New York Times* (March 30, 2003).

More Praise for Hyacinth for the Soul

Hyacinth for the Soul is a beautifully well-worked piece of imagination: ironic, lyrical, and elegant. Siegel's poems so often begin in daily living, poems that value the very simple or modest: what "abides" or "suffices." Sometimes somber, and sometimes happy, her poems shoot out into the cosmos and let us look at our living from that vantage. There are the pleasures of metaphor, where the parts of an idea suddenly condense or burst into a completely new structure that we recognize immediately: the "shape turning in the flame."

—Rosemary Deen
Poetry Editor, *Commonweal*

Joan Siegel's new collection, *Hyacinth For The Soul*, "pushes the door open on memory," determined to resurrect the "forgotten things," and to preserve all that will be lost, from her daughter's first words, to the "blue that smells of rain and colors the wild lupine." Siegel does not hesitate to "lift the heaviness left at her door" and transform it through the details of human experience and a love for the natural world into finely crafted lyrical poems of witness. Remembering becomes a legacy for her daughter and a generous gift to her readers.

—Frances Richey

Co-author of *Peach Girl: Poems for a Chinese Daughter* (Grayson Books/2002), Joan I. Siegel is recipient of the 1999 New Letters Poetry Prize and the 1998 Anna Davidson Rosenberg Award. Professor Emeritus of English at SUNY/Orange, she lives in New York's Hudson River Valley with her husband, daughter and cats.